# Zz

Bela Davis

Abdo
THE ALPHABET
Kids

**abdopublishing.com**

Published by Abdo Kids, a division of ABDO, PO Box 398166, Minneapolis, Minnesota 55439.
Copyright © 2017 by Abdo Consulting Group, Inc. International copyrights reserved in all countries.
No part of this book may be reproduced in any form without written permission from the publisher.

Printed in the United States of America, North Mankato, Minnesota.

102016
012017

 THIS BOOK CONTAINS
RECYCLED MATERIALS

Photo Credits: iStock, Shutterstock

Production Contributors: Teddy Borth, Jennie Forsberg, Grace Hansen

Design Contributors: Christina Doffing, Candice Keimig, Dorothy Toth

Publisher's Cataloging in Publication Data

Names: Davis, Bela, author.

Title: Zz / by Bela Davis.

Description: Minneapolis, Minnesota : Abdo Kids, 2017 | Series: The alphabet |
    Includes bibliographical references and index.

Identifiers: LCCN 2016943921 | ISBN 9781680809022 (lib. bdg.) |
    ISBN 9781680796124 (ebook) | ISBN 9781680796797 (Read-to-me ebook)

Subjects: LCSH: English language--Alphabet--Juvenile literature. | Alphabet
    books--Juvenile literature.

Classification: DDC 421/.1--dc23

LC record available at http://lccn.loc.gov/2016943921

# Table of Contents

## Zz

Cru**z** runs the ball to the end **z**one.

Zz

Zoe is at the zoo.

# Zz

**Z**ane put on a **snazzy** tie.

## Zz

Izzy **zz**ips up her **c**o**z**y coat.

# Zz

**Z**ion is a big park in Utah.

13

## Zz

**Z**uri **z**ooms on her sled.

14

# Zz

Ozzy likes to act zany.

## Zz

**Z**ara had a qui**z**. She got **z**ero wrong!

EXAM #1

NAME: Zara

Answer:

1. A ✓

2. D ✓

3. B ✓

4. C ✓

A ✓

6. C ✓

7. D ✓

8. B ✓

9. A ✓

10. C ✓

A+

19

Zz

What does **Z**ak see?

(a **z**ebra)

# More **Zz** Words

zebu

zinnia

zigzag

zucchini

# Glossary

**cozy**
snugly, warm, and comfortable.

**snazzy**
very stylish.

**zany**
very strange and silly.

# Index

## abdokids.com

Use this code to log on to abdokids.com and access crafts, games, videos, and more!

Abdo Kids Code:
**TZK9022**